# The Real First Lady

**CheVonceil Echols**

# The Real First Lady

Copyright 2021 CheVonceil Echols

All Rights Reserved. No part of the book may be reproduced in any form without written permission from Seymour Press.

ISBN: 978-1-938373-57-2

LCCN: 2021911503

Printed in the United States of America

© Seymour Press
   Lanham, MD 2021

*A*

*Memorabilia*

*Dedicated to my Loving Mother*

*Grace Marie Hill*

*From Her Daughter*

*Ethel Mae Bonner*

# Contents

Forward ............................. i
Preface ............................ ix
Portrait of a Family ................ 1
Early Years and Tragedies .......... 27
The Journey to Commit Murder ....... 35
The Morning Has Come ............... 55
A Living Legend .................... 61
Epilogue ........................... 79
The Author ......................... 81

## Forward

Thomas Gray, (1716-1771) the English poet, wrote a famous poem entitled The Bishop's Lady. Because a bishop was considered a lord of the church, he was addressed as My Lord Bishop and his wife was referred to as being the Bishop's Lady.

At a National Convocation during the 1960s Bishop Edwin Johnson, a former British subject, referred to Sister Ethel Mae Bonner playfully though respectfully as Lady Bonner. The nickname caught on like wildfire. Sister Bonner became known as the First Lady of the CHURCH OF OUR LORD JESUS CHRIST of Detroit, Michigan and the First Lady of REFUGE TEMPLE in New York City because her husband, Bishop William Lee Bonner was pastor of both .Thefact that this was the time of the Kennedy administrationand the fact that Jacqueline Kennedy was a prominent figure in her own right and was constantly being referredto by the press as the First Lady of the Nation all seemedto add fuel to the fire. When Bishop Bonner became the Presiding Apostle, people then began to refer to Sister Ethel Mae Bonner as the First Lady of the organization known as the CHURCH OF OUR LORD JESUS CHRIST OF THE APOSTOLIC FAITH, INC. What started as a bit of affectionate humor is about to develop into apostolic tragedy.

Miss Ethel Mae Smith (Bonner) at graduation from Hunter College in New York City.

Today, the habit of referring to and thinking of the pastor's wife as the First Lady is becoming more and more widespread. This is tragic because the last thing that a struggling church needs is a First or even a Second Lady. A church in its infancy or in the early stages of its development needs a mother; and the pastor's wife must be that mother even in her youthful years.

When the Pastor's wife refuses to play the role of the Mother of the Church or if she is denied the right to assume her role by the pastor, or by the missionaries, or by older members of the church, it becomes difficult for every woman in the church to know her place in relationship to the pastor and the flock; and it gives rise to great deal of emulation, jealousy, and strife (sometimes resulting in fisticuffs) within the ranks of the women of the church.

This casting of the pastor's wife in the role of Lady rather than Mother also has a very negative effect on the girls of the church. As they enter the stage of puberty, they begin to look upon the pastor's wife with eyes of contempt; and acting out of the impetuousness that is characteristic of youthfulness, they begin to treat the pastor' with familiarity that borders dangerously upon disrespect. This brazenness is often acted out in the very presence of the pastor's wife and worse still before the eyes of his children by birth provoking them to wrath. This girlish flippancy becomes a part of the behavioral pattern of young womanhood.

The Scriptures enjoins pastors not to lord it over God's people as is the custom of the Gentiles. To refer to the pastor as lord would be unapostolic and to refer to his wife as lady is equally as unapostolic. The Pastor's wife should strive to be not a First Lady but a Mother in Zion, and everyone should encourage her to do so.

Names are very important. For what we call a person determines to a large extent the way that person perceives of himself or herself. The way a person perceives of himself or herself determines to a large extent the way that person behaves or acts. In these present distressful times, it is imperative that the pastor's wife perceives of herself as the Mother of the Church and begins to act the part that the Gospel be not blamed.

Historically, the servant of all in the home has been the Mother; and among the parishioners in the church, there is no greater servant than the pastor's wife. A Lady, on the other hand is one who is not required to serve, but, instead, she is served.

There is no room in the New Testament Church for a First Lady. We all are servants of Christ and serve Him by serving each other. The man or the woman that is servant of all is greatest of all. The pastor's wife may never be appointed an office in the church, but she is the greatest woman in the church because she serves through suffering to an extent that no other woman does, can or should be expected to.

Women who have grown to maturity in the CHURCH OF OUR LORD JESUS CHRIST OF THE APOSTOLIC FAITH, INC. and have this testimony that they are truly rooted and grounded in the Apostolic Doctrine will also testify to the fact that they received their teaching from the pioneering women of whom Mother Grace Hill is one. Most of them are now deceased. At age ninety, she remains though confined to a wheel chair.

Mother Hill, in the sight of God, is the REAL First Lady not because she was the wife of a pastor and could lay claim to that title, only as long as he lived and continued to pastor, but because she permitted herself to be cast in the role of a Mother in Zion and played that role to the "endth" degree.

Mother Hill was Secretary for the State of New York from 1925-1947. She was the State Mother of New York from 1947-1953. During those years, there was no part of the state that she did not visit. When her strength began to fail, she selected six promising young women and in 1951 she began to train them to do her work calling them "State Mother Helpers." Among them were Sister Bessie Jones, Sister Beulah Turner, Sister Harriet Maloney, Sister Lillian McCarthy, Sister Gladys Towe and Sister Dorothy Anderson. In 1953, the State of New York was divided into four dioceses, these and other promising women became Diocesan Mothers.

Mother Hill was retired from active service to the organization but not from active service to God. She conducted Noon Day Prayer Service wherever she happened to be living; whether in the Carrie Lawson Residence (while her daughter was in Africa for three- and one-half years) or in her own apartment in the Lenox Terrace where she now lives.

God blesses her with excellent Home Attendants Janie Richardson, Gigi St. Charles and Nereida Gomez (who attend 24 hours per day, 7 days per week) and a devoted Personal Attendant, Sister Alberta Newton, who resides in the same building. He blesses her to maintain her financial independence from which she still pays her tithes.

At age ninety, with the help of thoughtful men of God like Elder Kenneth Lynton, Deacon Millard Sneak and Minister Curry, she is found in Sunday Morning Service each week seated in her wheel chair. When she talks with us, her speech is slow and her words few; but when she talks with God aloud, there is no impediment of speech whatsoever. Her mind is still sharp about the Scriptures and about the exact location of various passages of Scripture. She is blessed with many spiritual sons and daughters, the most loyal of whom is Bishop Thomas Richardson, who is in constant communication with her by mail and/or in person.

Last, but not least, Mother Hill is blessed to have a kind, loving, devoted and generous son-in-law in the person of Bishop William Lee Bonner, Presiding Apostle of the Church of Our Lord Jesus Christ of the Apostolic Faith, Inc., a devoted daughter affectionately known as Lady B, two grandchildren, William Lee Bonner Jr. and Ethel Mae Archer; four great grands, April, Lydia, Grace and William; and three brothers, Octave, George and Otho and their families.

If the One who spoke worlds into existence were to speak the words, "Will the REAL First Lady Please Stand," Mother Grace Hill would rise with majestic dignity from her wheel chair; and the rest of us, from the least to the greatest, would be privileged to remain seated.

*I present to you the biography of my mother.*

*Her Loving Daughter*
*Mother Ethel Mae Bonner*

**Pandora Williams State Mother of Michigan presents bouquet to Lady Grace Marie Hill.**

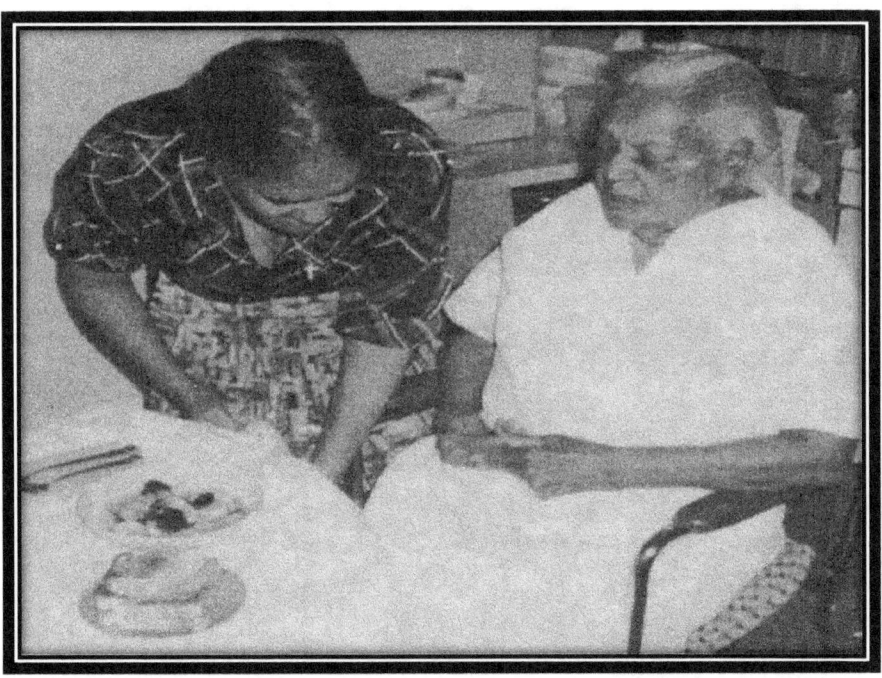

**Janie Richardson, devoted Home Attendant, lovingly serves breakfast to Lady Grace Marie Hill.**

# Preface
## March 3, 1982

This book is just a page, a caption, a glimpse of the life of Mother Grace Marie Jones Smith-Hill, born May 2, 1892. At this time Mother Hill is 89 years old residing in New York City. She was saved February 13, 1922, at the age of twenty-nine under the ministry of the late Bishop R. C. Lawson, with diabolical opposition from her husband Herbert John Smith.

On March 1, 1982, I had the opportunity and the great honor, at the invitation of her daughter Mother E. M. Bonner, to travel to New York City to assist in the writing of this biography. It was indeed a most inspiring and self-enlightening experience to have spent time, awake and asleep, in the presence of God's Chosen Women.

"To everything there is a season and a time to every purpose under the heaven." Mother Hill's life is one of ecclesiastical order. There was a time of birth: Herbert John, her son, and Ethel Mae, her daughter. A time of death: George Albert, her father, when she was but 18; Herbert John Smith, her husband, by suicide; and Herbert John, her son, at 11 years old in a traffic accident. There was a time to plant her life's hopes and dreams into little 4-year-old Ethel Mae, and a time to pluck up that which is planted. After the tragic death of her husband and son, Mother Hill and little Ethel literally started life over and it was to be a new beginning...

"You might say I stole away to the Lord, because I knew before I went into holiness that my husband was not going to like it; but I said in my heart, if it costs me my husband, my home, and my children I am going to get baptized in Jesus Name and receive the Holy Ghost, Lord. And it cost me every bit of that! So...there was a war between Herbert and me, a real war."

These words were spoken by Mother Hill in a taped interview given in May 1981 to her daughter, Mother Ethel Mae Bonner. Mother Bonner shared these thoughts shared in capsulizing Mother Hill's Journey. A Journey through the pinnacles of time.

"In her life there was "a time to weep and a time to laugh, a time to mourn, and a time to dance."" With these many emotions, I can only imagine the pain and uncertainties of losing three men in her young life. Her father to tuberculosis, her husband through suicide and her son to the fury of impetuous youth. Part of her mourned and part of her rejoiced, because through it all, she was alive and still surrendering her life to Christ.

"It was a time to cast away stones, and a time to gather stones together, a time to embrace;" and she did embrace, Ethel Mae only 4 years. She saw something in Ethel Mae that only a mother could see. It was "a time to refrain from embracing." Mother Hill did not harbor anger or bitterness towards her youth, her mistakes or toward life's wilderness journey.

Mother Hill said, "God must have something special for Ethel Mae, or he would have taken her life too, when he was cleaning out my house!"

"It was the worst of times and the best of times." Indeed, both of their lives are a Tale of Two [great] Cities. For them both it was "a time to get, and a time to lose; a time to keep and a time to cast away."

Oh! Time. Time that never ceases to exist. Time that never stops for anyone. "A time to rend, and a time to sow, a time to keep silence." Even now in her silence she still speaks.

It was "a time to hate..." all of what was evil and perverse, to hate sin enough to enter into the times of war that Mother Hill repeatedly speaks about when she said, "Then the war between Herbert and me was on... then the war began... so, we went to war and war it was. He hated my being in salvation so much so, he would have killed to prevent it - and he tried."

At long last for Mother Hill and Ethel Mae it became a time to love and a time of peace. These are the best of times, in these days and times.

"Behold my Mother, thou art fair my love, thou hast doves eyes. My beloved Mother is unto me as a cluster of camphire in vineyards of Engedi. Stay with me, comfort me, still me in thy silence, embrace me with the breath of thy life - let me live in you and twain our hearts " beat as one."

"For love is strong as death. Many waters cannot quench love, neither can the floods drown it..." So is Mother Bonner's love for her Mother. This Book is an expression of that love.

**Dr. CheVonceil Echols**

# Part One

# Portrait of A Family

# Herbert John Smith

## Evening of March 1, 1982

As I prepared for my journey into the life of Mother Hill, as a writer I needed to know what it was that attracted this young 18-year-old girl to the man who became her husband and "her enemy. Perhaps it was the same thing that attracts women today. "Was he a handsome man?" I asked.

Mother Bonner was four years old when he died and her image of him was lost in the pages of the trauma of seeing him leap from her bedroom window to his death. It was very late in the evening when we spoke, too late to begin my interview with Mother Hill. I was too excited to wait for her description I wanted to begin the research that evening upon my arrival.

I presented my request before the Lord in prayer. Lord please show me Herbert John Smith. This is what I saw:

Herbert John was of average height for a man in the 19th century, not extremely muscular but yet he possessed a sturdy physique. He had golden brown honey colored skin. He was smooth as black satin, not hairy. His teeth were like African ivory and when Herbert smiled, oh! his eyes lit up the hearts of many a young girl and sparkled with the mischief of a butterfly in flight! He was very handsome. In his dress he was very meticulous. As a valet to a king would be, Herbert was to himself. He was always neat and clean.

**Mother Hill's Family**

Back row: (from left to right) – Mother Hill's sister, Ethel Mae, her father, George; Mother (Grace, age 18) Hill; and her brother, Octave.
Front row: (from left to right) – Mother Hill's brother, Otho; her mother, Lillie Jones; and her brother, George.

Then I saw another Herbert; and he rose up in my mind's eye. He had an irascible nature, like wild fire and an army of untamed horses. A hint of danger appeared in the vision.

Hesitantly, the next morning I shared these thoughts with Mother Bonner. Was it all conjecture, from an inspired imagination? Mother Bonner agreed that this description was acceptable, in that she had no photographs to share.

March 3, 1982 Mother Bonner called her mother and we spoke with her concerning a description of Herbert John - This is an account of that interviews:

Mother Hills:

"He was brown skin, oh yes, he was medium· tall and slim and had small feet. Most of the time he had smooth skin. Sometimes he had a little mustache. I had a picture of him, and I did the wrong thing. I gave it to you (Ethel Mae) and I don't know what you did with it (Both Laughing) I thought maybe you'd like to have it."

(As though speaking to herself she says:)

"Yes, he was a nice looking brown-skinned fella. And always dressed like a... (Pause) He always dressed so well. Yes, he was very particular with his clothes. When he took them off, he folded them and put them on the back of the chair."

And

"He was quarrelsome. He could quarrel all night. He'd go to bed quarreling. He was jealous. Yes, very jealous. When he'd come home from work, he'd want to know what I had done that day, where I had gone, who I had seen and what I had said, while I was there. I met Herbert around 41st Street in New York. He lived down around 36th Street. I don't remember exactly where I met him to tell you the truth, but I was with a bunch of girls around 41st Street.

I knew he was nice looking and neat. He came from Saint Augustine, Florida."

The evening of March 3, 1982, Sister Mary Durant and myself accompanied Mother Bonner to the Bronx Church, pastored by Bishop Thomas Richardson where she had a speaking engagement. Mother Bonner asked Mother Wilhemina Wheatley to describe her father. This is an account of that interview:

Mother Wilhemina Wheatley:

"Yes, Lord Herbert was a beautiful man, a beautiful man. He was handsome alright. You never would have thought that a man who looked like he did, would do the things that he did, it was his handsome looks that attracted Grace."

(Shivering at the thought she says,)

"He was a dangerous man, fighting against God! You can't fight against God and win. NO SIR! Mother Lillie Jones, Grace's Mother had all of us praying for Grace. She knew Herbert was going to murder her or at least try. God SHOWED her that he had a gun."

(Shaking her head in dismay)

At this point Mother Bonner interjected:

"This is a great lesson for women, especially single women to note, that it is not in the looks of a man (emphatically she says) for even himself was beautiful. Marriage is an honorable estate. It is NOT to be played with. Once you consummate that vow, the only way out is DEATH! DEATH! The only way out is DEATH. It is not in the beauty of a man. So, in answer to the question Sister Echols posed to me, "What was it that attracted my mother to my father? It was the fact that he was a handsomeman."

January 30, 1923 Herbert John Smith after attempting to murder his wife, Grace Marie and mother-in-law, Sister

Lillie Jones, jumped five stories to his death, while his four-year-old daughter, Ethel Mae, watched.

# Grace Marie Jones

May 2, 1892 Grace Marie was born to George Albert and Amaryllia (Lillie) Jones. She was the eldest of six children. Octave Victor the eldest boy, Ethel Mae after whom Mother Bonner is named, George Thomas, Otho James, the youngest boy, and Josephine the baby who died at 15 months.

Grace was of medium build and height, soft-skinned, dove eyed and very pleasing to look at. She was quiet, yet there was a thread of silent strength woven into her character. In all that she set her mind to do, she did. Her actions were deliberate, not defiant. Grace was in awe of the wonderment of life. She viewed life with peripheral vision. She had so much to see, so much to do, in what must have seemed to her so little time and so little space.

Being the eldest child meant having many responsibilities very early in her young life. Her stature even at 15 was stately.

In 1907 at the age of 15, she held her first job working in Harlem as a maid for Miss Bernard, who made hats. It was also the year that Grace Marie graduated from the eighth grade.

In 1909, when she was 17, her father, George Albert Jones, became ill with tuberculosis. It was then that Grace Marie went to work for Mr. and Mrs. Willet in Flushing, New York. This is the family after whom Willets Point, the I.R.T. stop before Main Street, Flushing is named.

The Willett's House

Aunt Victoria and Uncle Tom Jenkins

## JOSHUA JENKINS' RITES HELD TODAY

Rites for Joshua Jenkins, Negro, who was sexton of the First Baptist Church of Flushing for 23 years, were held today in the church at Sanford avenue and Union street.

Mr. Jenkins died Monday in his 75th year. A resident of Flushing since childhood, he lived on Bud place.

He was born in Bayside, the son of the late Joshua and Cecelia Jenkins, who were also natives of Queens. His father owned one of the largest farms on Black Stump road.

Mr. Jenkins was descended from a long line of American farmers back to the 17th century. They settled in Middletown, Pa. His mother, Cecelia Jenkins, was a member of an old Jamaica family.

Mr. Jenkins attended the public schools of Flushing. He was baptized in Ebenezer Baptist Church.

He leaves his wife, Mary; three daughters, Mrs. Frances Harris, Mrs. Alyce French and Mrs. Matilda Mason; a son, David; three grandchildren; two brothers, Thomas and Charles, and a sister, Victoria.

The weight of helping to support her family also lended itself to her a soberness of mind and an aura of maturity.Grace carried herself as a lady before the time. This Iam sure is what attracted Herbert John to Grace Marie. She was a Princess then; as assuredly as she is a Queen now.

In 1910, when she was 18, her father died. It was May 3rd—Just a day after her birthday. Death has its way, of making one take stock of life, of goals,of direction of who one really is. I can only imagine, and not just as a writer, what she must have felt. For Iwas at the age of 19 when I lost a mother. Perhaps - shefelt as I did - who is Grace Marie? Why is Grace Marie? Where is Grace Marie? Dear God, if you really are, please,now is the hour to be... and perhaps she gathered up herloins and with strength mounted her hind's feet upon theof spices - And leaped to high places.

In 1910, at the tender age of 18, after her father's death, Grace Marie met and married Herbert John Smith.

In 1912, at the age of 20, she gave birth to her first child, a son, Herbert John.

In 1918, at the age of 26, on March 1st, her second child was born, a daughter, Ethel Mae.

In 1919, at the age of 27, Grace's Mother Amaryllia Lillie was saved through the ministry of Bishop R.C. Lawson at a tent meeting.

In 1922, at the age of 30, Grace was baptized in Jesus name, February 5th. On February 13th, she was filled with the Holy Ghost speaking in tongues.

"And the war between Herbert and me was on..."

January 30, 1923 at the age of thirty-one, Sister Grace Maria Smith was shot by her husband two times. Her mother was shot four times. "It was the hat," she said, "that saved my life – a hat."

# Herbert John Jr. (the son)

So little is known about young Herbert. first, Mother Bonner could not find any pictures of him. So again, I put my imagination to work. The old adage rang in my ears - "like father, like son."

Young Herbert was very much influenced by his father. He had his father's spirit. He wore his mannerisms like a king wears his crown. He was a wild buck. When he was let loose on the streets of New York, he ran as though he had been caged in like a leopard. I could only imagine that he too was very handsome, staunch, proud and mischievous.

The tension between Herbert Sr. and Grace mounted as young Herbert grew old enough to attend church. Her husband was Catholic. When Grace Marie expressed her desire to be saved, he was diabolically opposed to the idea. He was adamantly opposed to any religion that was not Catholicism. "If it was not Catholicism, it was not a religion." So, they battled; and Grace eventually got Herbert to agree to let Herbie go to a church near their apartment; but she was never to mention Salvation or the Holy Ghost in his house.

Young Herbert heard his father say, "I told you once, woman, my children gonna be Catholic. I'm Catholic and I'm gonna die Catholic. They ain't goin to no holy rolling Church, they're already sanctified! Your mama is still talking about that holiness church, I don't wanna hear no more 'bout' it, Ya hear? That's final!"

From that moment on, young Herbert began to side with his father. And when they sent him out to church, he would play hooky.

Herbert Jr. had an unruly spirit and after his father attempted to kill his grandmother and mother and then succeeded in killing himself, Herbert began to personify, at the young age of ten, a living death.

February 1924 at the age of 11, one year and one month after his father died, young Herbert left the house one day and ran like a leaf being blown by the wind in four directions at once.

In the whirlwind of his impetuous youth, he hitched a ride on the back of a bus; and in the snow he slid from corner to corner delighting no doubt, in his mischief. And then suddenly, without notice, he leaped off into the path of an approaching taxi cab and he was smashed to death between the two.

# Ethel Mae

Ethel Mae was born March 1, 1918. She was the apple of her father's eye. She was the one and only one that he delighted in.

She was very young and tender. She was the stalwart of her family even at four. Loved deeply by her father, cherished by her mother, probably catered to by her grandmother, and entertained by her older brother, I envision her as the center of the family's attention (if you please).

Much like her mother in her girlish ways, she had an "I must do" mentality. She grew to be strong and possessed the strength of an army of ten thousand, yet she has the ways of a woman. Too few women possess both qualities simultaneously, strength and femininity.

If you look into her eyes you don't see the future, or her dreams, not even a trace of pain. No, it is not in her eyes—but it is in her words. Her life are her words in action.

After her father died, Mother Bonner had expressed to me in one of the very first interviews, that she could remember very little, almost nothing of her childhood. She had no images, no memories, no feelings; yet she had a need to know. Now, at this time in her life, she had a need to be able to reach inside and touch her own infirmities, to realize the pain, perhaps even at long last to cry, and know the reason for tears.

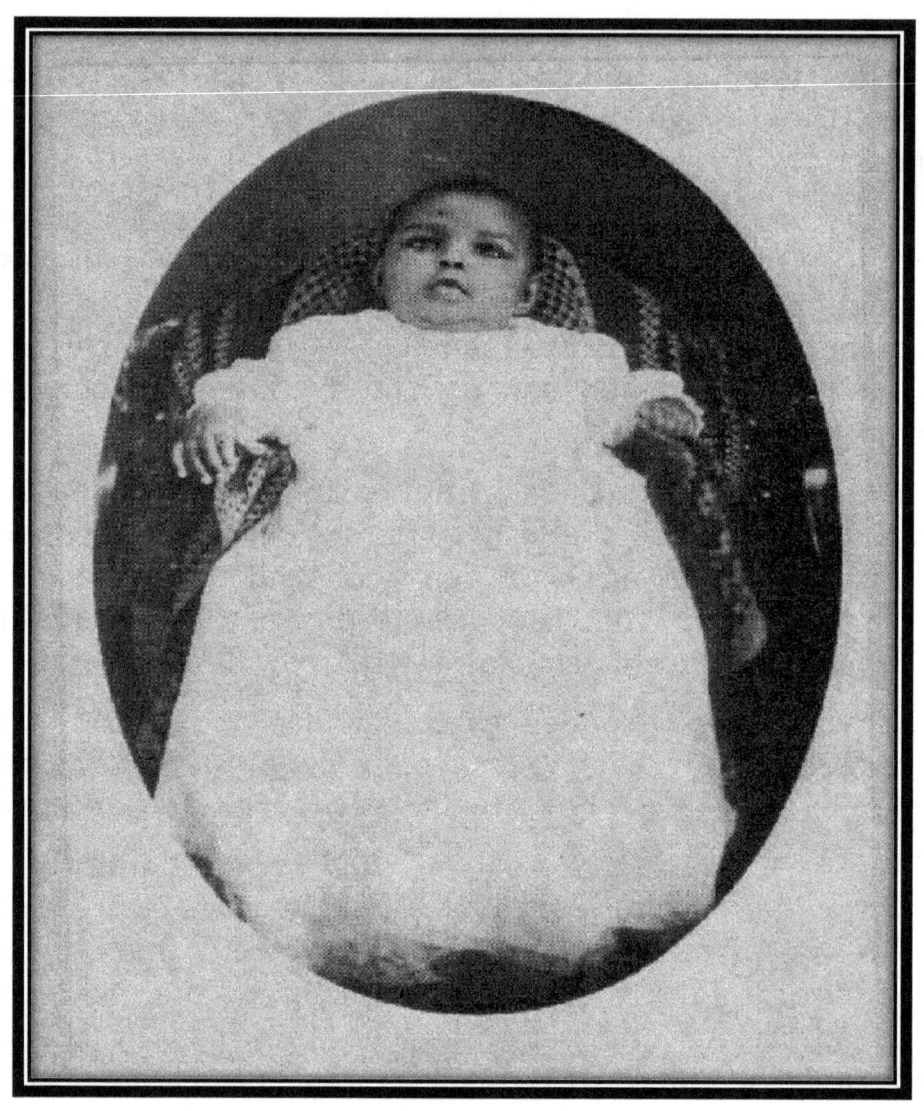

On January 30, 1923 Ethel Mae was outside playing, She had fallen down and young Herbert had brought her upstairs crying, After Grace Marie comforted her she sent her to the living room to play, Not too long after, a heated argument between Herbert and Grace grew louder --

Then... the gun shots

Then... the screaming

Then... footsteps running

Then... more gun shots

Then... more screaming

Then...silence

Then with bright eyes widened Ethel Mae popped her head out from behind the victrola where she had been hiding-not knowing where Mommie was, not knowing who Daddy was playing-the good guy or the bad guy...

She saw him enter her bedroom and before her innocent eyes untouched by life's cruel stains, she watched him jump out of her window.

She was frozen with fear and for many months Ethel Mae was afraid to sleep in her room. The older she got, the further away she grew from that day; and the memories of her childhood were buried with her father.

This writer says she is beautiful in every way. All of her good works and criticized efforts make her what she is-a stalwart, the nuclei, the center.

Mother Hill's words keep ringing in my ears:

"God must have had something special for Ethel Mae, or He would have taken her life too, when he was cleaning my house out!"

He did! and this writer says: he still does!

Mother Hill's Sister, Ethel Mae Jones, Harris Boone, after whom "Lady B" was named is shown as a young girl (below) and a married woman

# Amaryllia Lillie Jenkins-Jones

Grandma Lillie, as she was called before salvation, was a hard-working woman. She had six healthy children, and a hard working but ailing husband.

She was the driving force that birthed the spirit of these women of whom I speak the root of determination to survive against all of the odds the unbreakable twig. Hers was a no-nonsense life.

Grandma Lillie was the sunflower of 131 street touching everything and everybody along the way; and what she touched was set on fire. For it was she whom God entrustedto carry the word of truth to Grace Marie and to Ethel Mae. The plan and purpose of God cannot be thwarted by mere human intent.

It was in 1919 that Grandma Lillie had heard of a man who preached like John the Baptist, taught like Paul, and lived like Christ. He was young and fiery. His name was Elder R.C. Lawson. It was at a tent meeting that she heard the gospel preached and accepted it verbatim.

Upon being baptized and filled, Sister Lillie Jones began to witness to her daughter. She was a faithful witness. Never would Sister Jones let anyone come in her presence and not hear about salvation. Through her testimony, not only Grace and her own younger sister came to Christ but many others as well.

Her husband never received the Holy Ghost; but he was a good man who loved his family and who was proud of his family. He always told his children, "If you make your bed hard, lay in it." He would say, "Show me the company you keep, and I'll tell you who you are." He died May 3, 1910.

Sister Jones grew in faithfulness to her calling and adorned the title of Mother Lillie Jones. She was a good woman and a good mother. She was very handy with a needle. Although she went to night school to learn the techniques of drafting, crocheting, embroidery and knitting, Mother Jones had very little education.

Mother Lillie was hated and despised by Herbert Smith; so much so, that he plotted to kill her.

-----"She was a Praying Woman,"-----

Mother Wilhemina Wheatley gives this account:

> Mother Jones had come to the Church and asked everybody to pray for Grace. She (Grace) was newly saved. Herbert had just come back from Florida and the Lord had revealed to Mother Jones, in prayer, that he had a gun.
>
> You see Mother Jones was a praying woman. She fasted for so long that her skin had turned a different color, and she was not the same. Herbert had a murderous spirit and she knew it, God revealed it to her. He had a gun.

# Part Two

# Early Years and Tragedies

**Mother Bonner Speaks:**

March 1, 1982<br>Her birthday

There were four deafening gun shots each one piercing my memory. I was afraid. I suppose fear would have been an instinctive reaction. I don't remember much on purpose. It was a traumatic experience for a four-year-old child. There is so much concerning my childhood that I don't remember. I have always felt that there was a possibility that I forced many things from my memory, because they were too painful for me to remember. I realize now that there is almost an urgent need to find out all I can. The extermination of one's childhood is not conducive to good mental health. I want to begin to piece together the early history of my life so that I can acquire a better understanding of why I react as I do to certain situations in this particular season of my life. I have a need to remember what I have internalized.

# The Year 1910

New York was never more beautiful than in 1910. As usual it was busy, people bustling from pillar to post. Young folks of today would have really gotten a kick out of the modesty of the women of yesteryear; and Grace Marie was no different. She was 18 and today was her wedding-day. She was marrying one of the most sought-after young men who used to parade up and down 41st street. No one could deny that it looked like love, acted like love, and felt like love to the newly wedded Smiths.

Grace had had it in her mind to get married when she turned 18; and she did just that! She didn't have a church wedding; and her mother didn't find out she was married until after she had done it. It was just like Mother Lillie to be happy for Grace, although her stomach ulcer disagreed.

Perhaps Grace thought marriage was getting support for her family now that her father had died.

There was something else in the air, not discernible through mere human eyes. It was beneath the heart and above the soul. This feeling, this thing had no dwelling place as of yet...in the young lives of these two lovers.

As with most newly wedded couples, they were happy, inseparable and unknowing. Grace was a New York City girl; Herbert was a Southern Florida boy. Grace was a sometime Baptist, Herbert was a devout, to a limit, Catholic. Grace was the eldest of six children who started working as a maid at the age of 15 making $3.00 a week. Herbert had one brother living in Florida and a sister named Helen Finney living in New York. Grace knew the importance of family planning and the grave responsibility of being a wife and a mother. After her father died, she became a very vital part of the family lifeline. She helped keep the family alive and worked hard. Herbert did provide the necessities, like, food, clothing and shelter; but he gave little of himself in love, nurturing and affection.

But they were married now –

> "For better or for worse
> For richer or for poorer
> In sickness and in health
> Til death do us part."

## 1912 - 1918

Herbert and Grace had two beautiful children. They were relatively comfortable, by no means rich and in no way poor. They had their differences and it always seemed to be concerning the same thing, Religion! If it wasn't Catholicism, it wasn't. It just wasn't! There was a ruling in those days about signing a statement that any children born of a Catholic and non-Catholic would be indoctrinated in Catholicism. Grace didn't like the ideaof signing any statement. So, Herbert allowed Herbie to go to a church near their apartment, King's Chapel pastored by Mother Susan Lightford.

Herbert loved Ethel Mae. Before she was born, he used to be so jealous, having to know every move Grace made. Little Ethel seemed to soften him. He used to say that she was the prettiest thing in seven states. I'm sure she has often wondered, why just seven states. Perhaps it is because it is God's perfect number.

Herbert use to question the children about what their mother had done that day. Where they had gone, whom they had seen. His major concern was Grace's visiting her mother who was just hearing about salvation. He wanted no part of it.

Herbert and Grace constantly battled in word wars. He resented her mother, perhaps resented being married.

Soon, something in the air, not discernible through human eyes, began to rise up into the heart and deep down into the soul. That feeling that thing that had no dwelling place in the young lives of' these two lovers - NESTED.

It was a balmy day, Grace busied herself as usual getting everybody up and out to school and to work. She prayed, then faced the day ahead.

There was something different about this day in the year 1919. Grace's mother, Lillie had been to a tent meeting. It was set up by a young fiery minister. His name was Elder R.C. Lawson. He preached like a 'wild man' - crying out as though in the wilderness. His voice was loud; and the words he spoke echoed like the warning of' a fog horn through the clouded mist. **REPENT! REPENT! REPENT!**

That evening at the revival, Lillie Jones became Sister Lillie Jones. She was baptized in Jesus' name and filled with the Holy Ghost.

Sister Lillie lived at 15 E 131$^{st}$ Street and Herbert and Grace lived at 7 E 131$^{st}$ Street. There were about eight houses between them (they still stand today, although boarded up). Both lived on the top floor in each building. So, Grace and Sister Lillie developed a habit of crossing over the roofs instead of making the five flights which equaled 20 flights by the time they went back and forth and up and down.

Sister Lillie was the first in the family to receive the Holy Ghost. Naturally she wanted to share this good news about salvation with her children. She began to witness to Grace and the Word began to take effect.

After Sister Lillie got saved the relationship between Herbert and his mother-in-law grew even more tense than before. They never did have a good relationship anyhow. Herbert had a domineering personality and so did Sister Lillie so the two always seemed to disagree. If Herbert said it was cold, Sister Lillie said it was cold, but not that cold! If Sister Lillie said it was too expensive to buy clothes when you can make your own, Herbert would say he didn't like homemade clothes.

When Sister Lillie said, "You need to repent and be baptized in the name of Jesus Christ for the remission of YOUR sins." From that moment on, he did not want Grace's mother even near the house, the children, Grace or himself, he made it clear and meant what he said.

From 1919-1921 the friction was intense between Grace and Herbert. He would go out and not come home. He was constantly fussing. That temper began to flare up like the nostrils of a mad bull.

Grace was almost at her wits end, nervous, fearful of his temper, concerned about the children. Yet she had a strong desire to hear the testimony of her mother. She was for several years a woman torn between two loves.

It was November 1921, Sister Lillie had obviously been praying again. Whenever she prayed, God moved heaven, earth, the stars, the moon, the rivers and Herbert.

Herbert had received an emergency phone call from Florida. His brother had taken ill, and he had to leave New York as soon as possible. His sister lived downstairs. So, he asked her to help Grace and keep aneye on things.

It was just beginning to snow. It was the kind of cold that sent chills up the back and around the shoulders, and shivers shook the body as a bird does waterfrom its back.

After Grace saw Herbert off, she went back to the apartment on 131st street. It was dark, cold and had a damp feeling. The children were with Grandma Lillie. It was quiet. Herbert had left a warning against the Holy Ghost in every room.

The apartment that once rang with the laughter of young love and filled with the prosperity that children can bring was now mocking her. It was as though the demons that Herbert left behind held the keys to her happiness.

Grace fell on her knees and cried out to God for deliverance, for peace, for salvation. Little did she know that the prayer her mother had prayed had come to pass. The stumbling block was moved for a space of time. It was the Red Sea experience for Grace.

It was in the year 1921 that Grace began her journey from Egypt to Canaan.

1922 was the turning point for Grace Marie in many respects. She was thirty years old. She had been married for twelve years. She had two beautiful children and a supportive mother.

Grace was at one of the many crossroads that she would face on life's journey. She had a very important decision to make. A decision that could change her whole life or cost it.

Life is full of choices, and the challenges of being a woman no doubt excited Grace Marie especially a woman at thirty. You choose to be up, choose to be down, choose to be single, choose tobe married, choose to be proud, to be humble, choose to be a friend or an enemy. It is because of the free will that God gives us that we can choose to be anything that want to be. Making a choice is taking a chance.

AND... take a chance she did.

## *February 5 — 13, 1922*

It would have been just another ordinary day in New York City. The usual routine took place. Grace got up very early that day. She and her mother had had a long talk the night before about getting baptized in Jesus name. Sister Lillie tried to reassure Grace that no matter what Herbert threatened to do, God was able and would not fail. I can almost hear her saying,

> For we wrestle not against flesh and blood, but against principalities, against powers, against the rulers of the darkness of this world, against spiritual wickedness in high places (Ephesians 6:2).

The time to make a decision was now while Herbert was away. God let it be so. I can imagine that Sister Lillie might have said, "Time is wasting child. That man will be home any day and you'll be right back where you started from only worse and still powerless."

After Grace got the children breakfast, she hurried Herbert Jr. off to school. She began to think about the conversation concerning the baptizing. The words no doubt kept ringing in her ears:

> "What shall we say then? Shall we continue in sin? Shall we continue in sin? Continue in sin; Continue in sin; sin... sin..."

She was startled when she came to herself. Her sister-in-law had been knocking at the door. As Grace opened the door, Helen said, "Looks like a letter from Herbert." She handed Grace the letter. Grace grew quiet and still. It was from Herbert. As Grace opened the letter her hands trembled. This was the spirit of fear he had left as guard over his home.

She came to the part that caused her to tremble all the more. It read:

"Is your Mama still talking to you about that holiness church? Have you been going? I told you once, my children gonna be Catholics. They ain't 'goin' to no holy rolling church. They already sanctified! You hear me woman? When I get back, I don't want to hear no more talk about it. That's final!"

I can only imagine that while she read the letter, the words, "shall we continue in sin" kept ringing in her ears; and at the same time, she could no doubt hear his voice in her mind.

Mother Bonner gave this account, (as told to her)

My mother took the letter and walked quietly into the kitchen and placed the letter on the chair and knelt before the Lord. My mother, I don't believe had ever read II Kings 18, when Hezekiah had received a letter saying Jerusalem would be delivered to the Assyrians. He prayed before the Lord, and said, "Lord bow down thine ear, and hear: open, Lord thine eyes, and see. I beseech, thee save thou us out of his hands that all thy kingdoms of the earth may know that thou art the Lord God, even thou only."

So my mother prayed, they tell me, and she said to the Lord: "Lord God of Abraham, Isaac, and Jacob, when I answer this letter, I want not only to be able to say for a surety that I am going to the house of God to praise your name, but Lord my God, I want to say, that I am baptized and Filled with the gift of the Holy Ghost with the sign and evidence of speaking in tongues, and with every intent of my heart. I will continue in the way."

"Then Isaiah the son of Amoz sent to Hezekiah, saying thus saith the Lord God of Israel, that which thou hast prayed to me, I have heard."

Likewise, also, God heard my mother's prayer and on February 5, 1922 she was baptized and on February 13, 1922 she was filled and continues steadfast at age ninety strong in the Apostolic Doctrine.

So, you see, it was not just another ordinary day. It was an extraordinary day. It was the day of choices, of crossing over to the other side, of passing through the Red Sea, of leaving Egypt.

"What shall we say then? Shall we continue in sin, that Grace may abound? God forbid. How shall we, that are dead to sin, live any longer in it? For he that is dead is freed from sin…Freed from sin…Freed. Freed." Grace Marie Smith was FREE!

It was April 1922 seven months later. Herbert came home. His brother had died and was buried. Grace also had died and was buried with Christ through baptism.

And the war was on.

# Part Three

# The Journey to Commit Murder

# January 1923

From the April of 1922 to January 30, 1923 Herbert fought constantly with the now-SISTER GRACE SMITH. He was infuriated with his mother-in-law and he had changed so much. The anger he had accumulated was almost visible. His eyes were wild, his jaw was always clenched, his fist only being held back from Grace by the mercy of God.

Mother Wilhemina Wheatley gives this account:

My experience with Herbert John happened one time when Mother Jones had asked everybody to pray for Grace. She was newly saved. Herbert had just come back from Florida and had this gun. He was upset and started keeping Grace and Ethel Mae in the house. He wouldn't let them go nowhere. He forbid her to go out of the house.

Some of the old mothers told me to go over and see how Grace was and to talk to Herbert. So, I went. While I was walking over there, I heard this voice say, "Don't you go! It kept on so strong, that I stopped right in the middle of the street and said, "Who is this Lord?" I knew it was God. So, I went back to the church.

As I came in the door, the sisters said, "What are you doing back so soon?" I told them what the Lord had said. So, I stayed at the church and prayed, while they went to see Grace.

When they finally came back, they came back crying, Herbert had treated them so badly, He said, "I don't respect you; I don't respect what you stand for; I don't respect your God, or what you say. This is my house, my wife and my business. The only thing I do respect, and the only thing that keeps me from kicking you both down five flights of stairs is the gray hair on your head." Then he said, "Get out," and slammed door.

(Mother Wheatley, as though vividly remembering says:)

"Praise the name of Jesus! Thank God, I listened to his voice, Because if I had gone to see Grace, I could have been kicked down five flights of stairs. You see I had not one gray hair!"

At that point we approached Bishop Lawson and we all prayed. Mother Lillie had told us that Herbert John had a murderous spirit. She had prayed and fasted so long her skin changed colors. Herbert was dangerous. Mother Lillie said God showed her that Herbert had brought a gun back with him from Florida, and that he had planned to kill her or at least he was going to try. You never would have thought, that a handsome man like that could be like that. It's not in the looks of a man, blessed be thename God."

### *January 29, 1923*

Grace was getting Herbie ready for church. She had been attending Refuge Temple. She was trying to hurry him quicklyand quietly so as not to awaken Herbert and to avoid thequarreling she knew he would start. Well, as the devil would have it, he woke up. Fortunately, right after Herbiehad left.

He wanted to know what was going on. Grace explained; and he hit the ceiling. He said if Herbie was going anywhere, it was to a Catholic church. They quarreled. They quarreled about Catholicism vs Holiness. They quarreled about the baptism, Salvation, her dress, her hair, her mothering and finally at last about her mother, Sister Lillie Jones, "the real culprit," he said, "to the whole mess." From marital problems to you name it. He hated her mother.

He got dressed and said he was going right to that church and get Herbie. After several hours he came back angrier than when he left. Herbie wasn't at church and hadn't been coming.

Mother Bonner speaks:

"I believe my brother, from what my mother told me, was rebelling against her, because of my father. He couldn't serve two masters, so he chose to follow my father. He began to play hooky from church and from school."

Herbert was angry because he couldn't find Herbie. He began to yell at Grace; and finally, he raised his hand to her and struck her. Ethel Mae tried to defend her mother. Crying, confusedly she said, "Don't you hit my mother! Don't you hit my mother!" Ethel Mae loved her father and he loved her; yet the threads of all their lives were being ripped apart.

Hebert Jr. was out in the streets doing who knows what. Ethel Mae, four, was confused as to what was wrong with Mommie crying and Daddy yelling. Grace was determined to" live for God regardless of the consequences. I can imagine that she must have remembered the scripture that says,

*"Who shall separate us from the love of Christ? Shall tribulation, or distress, or persecution, or famine, or nakedness, or peril, or sword? As it is written, For thy sake we are killed all the day long; we are accounted as sheep for the slaughter. Nay, in all these things we are more than conquerors through him that loved us. For I am persuaded that neither death, nor life, nor angels, nor principalities, nor powers, nor things present, nor things to come, Nor height, nor depth, nor any other creature shall be able to separate· us from the love of God, which is in Christ Jesus Our Lord."*

(Romans 8)

Herbert was determined to separate Grace from the great challenge of this scripture. He thought the power of a bullet was greater than the powerof God.

*January 23, 1923 (evening)*

After Herbert had attacked Grace and frightened Ethel Mae into defending her, it grew dangerously silent and remained so until the sun was overshadowed by the moon.

There was no laughter. It was lost in the crevices of a stony heart, and joy had mounted itself upon wings of the vows Herbert and Grace had made –

"Til death do us part
or
For as long as we both shall live:"

When Herbie finally came home from playing hooky from church, both Herbert and Grace avoided scolding him. They had argued all day. What more could be expected of this 11-year-old child than to lose himself in his parents' turmoil. He was home, safe – or so it seemed.

That evening Grace gathered the children together and told Herbert that she was spending the night at her mother's. He didn't like the idea; but he couldn't stop her. She told him that what they needed was a space of time apart to see things clearly. So, she left.

That night, at her mother's house, they prayed; and during that prayer, the Lord spoke to Sister Lillie. When they had ended the prayer, Sister Lillie took Grace by the hand and asked her if she trusted God, believed that He could make her enemies to stumble and fall? She said, no doubt, "Greater is He that is in you, than He that is in the world."

"Grace," she said, "The Lord told me that Herbert is going to try to kill you and me. He told me that you must get out of that house for good. So tomorrow you take a policeman with you to get some things for you and the children."

# The Spirit of Death
## The Morning of January 30, 1923

Grace Marie and Herbert lived on the top floor of a railroad flat. Mother Bonner drove me by the apartment house on 131st which is now boarded up. She describes it as simply a railroad apartment. It went from room to room straight from the front door to the back door. The following page give a better description of the layout.

It is important at this point for the reader to imagine the scene I am about to describe. For it was on this day, January 30, 1923 at the home of Herbert and Grace Smith that an act of attempted murder was about to take place. It was a day that had been unrehearsed but expected as inevitable.

It was still snowing as the sun began to rise in the early hours of the morning. Grace had wrestled all night with the words her mother had spoken, "Kill us, try to kill us." It was unimaginable that Herbert would even dare point a gun at Grace. It wasn't like him. Sure, he was not acting himself. "It was the pressure of the days and times we were living." Then, just as soon as her mind heard "kill us," a voice whispered, "Trust, trust me, trust me now."

She got up in the still of the morning and gazed out of the window. There was a fear in the street, a silence, like death lurking. A chill ran down her spine. Grace may have looked back on her life in retrospect, and thought, Lord, I'm 31 years old, with two children and a stranger for a husband. All I ever wanted was to be happy, to give my love and to be loved. Now, I am your child, I am in your care and I do trust and even more than trust I believe.

It was around noontime Grace had contacted the police department for an escort home to gather the children and her belongings. As they approached the fifth flight, the officer seemed more and more reluctant, "I had to decide whether to go in or not. Fear gripped my body; but God gave me courage - so I knocked on the door."

For some reason Herbert knew someone was with me, he said, who's with you? Whoever it is, let them come in too!" There was a snarl in that invitation. When he realized it was the police, he got angry and began to curse. I believe he wanted it to be Mama, so he could kill us both. He yelled at the officer, that I wouldn't be no safer in the street, if he had had evil intentions. Those were his words. By saying that, I believed it meantthat he did not have evil intentions. So the officer leftme there alone; but I was not alone. "For greater is He that is in me, than He, that is in the world."

I came in and began to pick up the children's things. They were outside playing in the snow. Herbert was quiet at first. Then he began to talk kind of sweet and gentle almost apologetic. He sounded like what that old serpent musthave sounded like talking to Eve. I was very careful withmy words. I would feel him leading me into an argument. He wanted me to reconsider leaving; but I had always said,that I would stay as long as I could, but if he ever struck me then I would leave. So, I was leaving.

While I was home, my mother told me later, that the Lord had showed her, that I was in danger, even though we were just talking like husband and wife. So, she got herself ready to come over. She started to tell a neighbor, Sister Hopkins that she was going, but the Lordsaid," No! She'll tell you not to go." Sister Hopkins lived across the hall from her. Then her thought was to tell Sister Lee. Again, the Lord said no to that too! Hetold her to go alone, even in the face of death.

Just before my mother came up to my apartment she stopped at Herbert's sister's apartment, She was the caretaker of the building. She stopped to tell her very emphatically that her brother, Herbert was going to commit murder that very day.

Mama came up, but knocked on the door adjacent to my apartment, being directed by the Lord all the way. Herbert and I were still talking, I was still packing. I heard the knock on the other apartment door but hadn't made the connection that it was Mama.

Herbert paced back and forth mumbling under his breath, looking out the window, down at the kids - telling me they need a father, that church, your Mama, you, you're ruining this marriage. Just as I was about to respond, he noticed that Ethel Mae had fallen off of the sled and was crying. He yelled down to Herbie to bring her upstairs. I asked him not to talk about the subject in front of the children. Just then, I heard Ethel Mae crying. I went to the door and at the very same time, Mama opened the door to the apartment adjacent to mine, and said, "What happened?"

It was the Lord. She came in with the kids and began to comfort Ethel Mae. Mama's very presence changed Herbert's whole attitude. He was visibly annoyed, even though she just spoke and helped the children take off their wet clothes.

Herbert and I went to the front end of the house to talk. Mama and the children were in the kitchen. The door was locked, and the key was removed from the front door. The only way out was four rooms back to the kitchen. It was a long walk for it was a railroad flat.

After Mama came in Herbert went to get his coat as if he were going out. That's when we went up front. He was asking me to stay with him. He wanted us to stay together for the children's sake. He said, "You can take one half of the house to live in and I'll take the other half. Just don't leave," he said. There was no way I could consent to those terms. I remember the scene so well, I played it over and over again in my mind. I looked straight in Herbert's eyes, and said," When I married you I was only 18 years old; now I'm 31. I made up my mind then, that I would stay with you, but I would also leave when and if I had to - and stay out. And last night (January 29, 1923) I had to get out (after he hit her) and now I'm gonna stay out."

## Conjecture

It was snowing that day. It was cold that hour. It was quiet that minute. As the author, I can only imagine that this was the feeling, the spirit, the mood of the time. The time just before the plan to kill. For Herbert it was a time to kill.

In Herbert's coat pocket he had a gun. This is why, when Mama came in, he went to get his coat. After I told him I could not and would not stay, he became enraged - like a mad man. He jumped up and started to yell, and stomp his feet. He pointed his finger in my face. The whole house shook with anger and hate. All of a sudden, the children came running up to the front of the house but chose to hide behind the furniture. Herbert was yelling so loud, that his sister came running upstairs. The way to enter the house was through the kitchen door. The back door was at the front end. Mama opened the door and they both started up to the front sitting room.

Herbert was so unpredictable it was hard for me to tell how to deal with him. His sister tried to get him to stop fussing. By this time Herbert tried to jump at me. There was a brief moment of fear and loss of balance. His sister jumped between the two of us and pushed him back. She kept walking towards him. He would back away. She would say, "Herbie, what's wrong with you? This is your wife. You're frightening the kids! Are you crazy?" Still walking towards him, she backed him all of the way from the sitting room to the kitchen door, four rooms back.

At that moment, I sensed the purpose of all of it. The Lord had wanted us out of the front room and in the kitchen. I didn't know what Herbert was going to do. I still did not know he had a gun. Only his sister could have pushed him that far. As we entered the kitchen, the Lord told me to grab my hat and put it on - I did.

"A hat saved my life."

## Conjecture

Mama, at that same moment, told me very calmly and quietly, as though not to startle me, to open the door and run. Immediately, without question or pause, I ran to the head of the stairs. I was concerned that the children were still in the house. The Lord said, "Trust me now!" Just as I was about to descend the stairs, I turned to look back for Mama...

And in the doorway stood this tall, brown, handsome man, neatly dressed, with a half-smile on his brown lips and a mischievous glint in his eyes. For one split second I saw a flash back of Herbert saying, "Til death do us part." It was then that I saw pointed straight at my head the barrel of his gun...

He fired one shot.

I turned without thinking and ran down the stairs screaming. The shot rang out loud and full of hate and venom. The bullet hoping for bloodshed went straight through my hat. I screamed louder, still running down three flights of stairs. He ran forward and fired his second shot. I screamed, "Murder! Murder! Murder!" The neighbors were peeking through the doors. I was trembling so, that my knees were actually knocking; and I almost fell down the stairs - I was so blinded with my own emotions and trauma that I did not know Mama was running behind me.

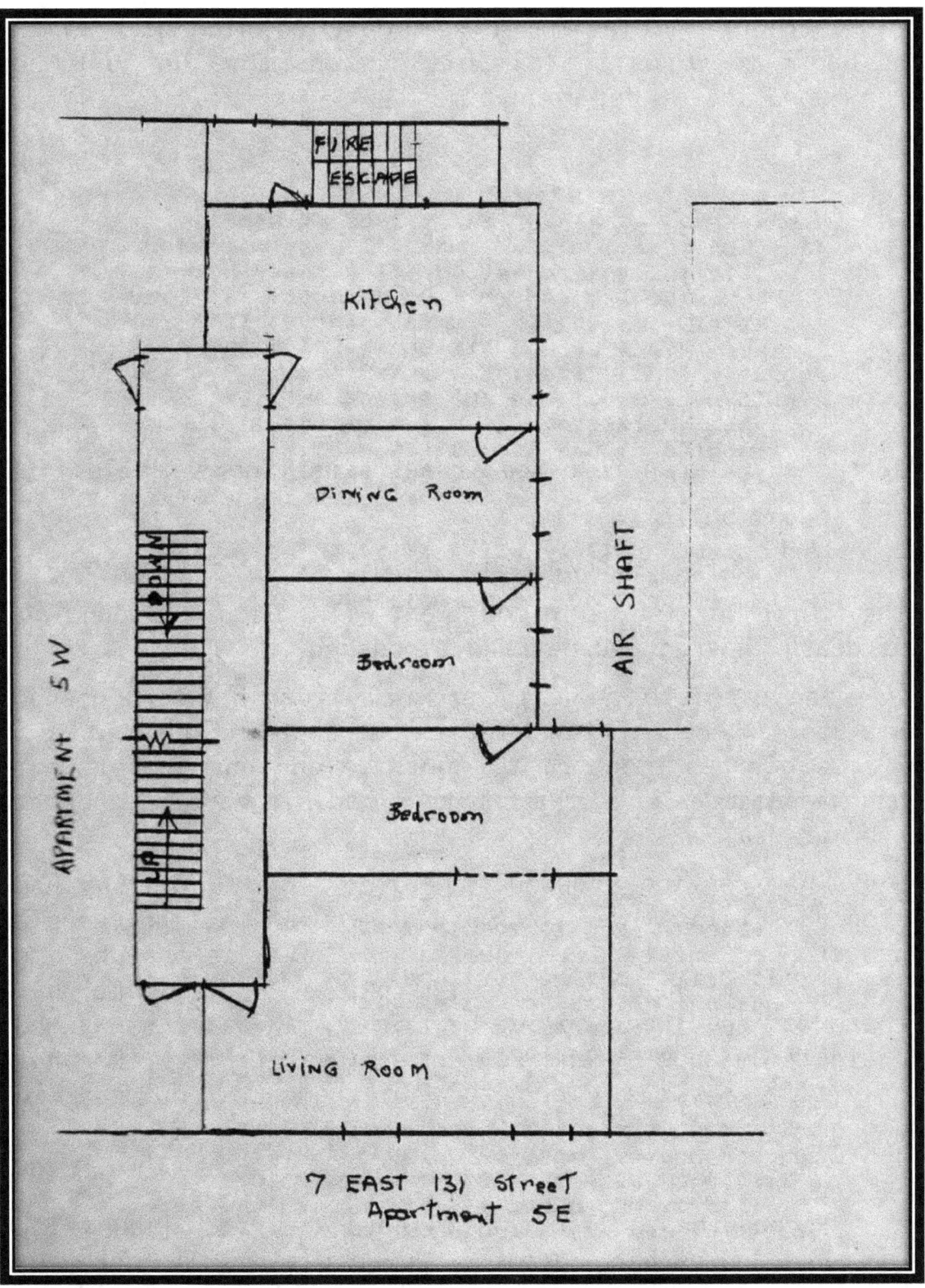

Herbert shot at me twice. After missing both times he began to focus and aim his gun on Mama. He followed her, shooting at her four times.

BANG!

BANG!

BANG!

BANG!

The first bullet hit her in the side, I heard her scream out, I ran into the street screaming for help.

The second bullet hit Mama.

The third bullet ricocheted.

The fourth, praise be to God, went wild. Each one sounding of death, hatred, murder and bloodshed.

Mr. Singleton, who lived on the fourth floor, opened his door on the third and fourth gun shot and grabbed Mama inside his apartment. I was outside and unaware of what had happened. I knew that Herbert had hit Mama. I thought she was dead.

The shooting stopped. All grew silent. The sun had stopped shining. The snow too had stopped falling. People had stopped to stare, to question. It was as though time itself and my heart had ceased to be. - I was hurt; but there was no blood, no cut or bruise. My heart had ached inside from anguish and the unknown possibility that not only Mama was dead, but the children too could be in danger.

"Trust me now."

Someone had called the police and sirens were in the distance approaching. From my understanding Herbert went back into the apartment where the children were hiding. He locked the door.. and never came out again...

Mother Hill stated that "Ethel Mae then had run to the front room and hid behind the Victrola. Little Herbie then eleven hid himself under the bed in his room. Herbert was like a wild man, blinded with rage. I believe he must have been looking for the children to do what, I don't know, but God hid them and blinded him. He tried no doubt, to shoot himself but all of the bullets were gone. He took himself into the children's room" Throwing things and cursing he went to the window.

## Conjecture

Herbert must have heard the sirens, saw the crowd and panicked all the more. He opened the window. People he knew called up to him, but his rage had deaf ears. The police had not yet arrived, nor the ambulance for Mama. Everything happened so quickly, yet it seemed as though hours had passed...

Suddenly without warning, I heard people screaming, "Don't do it! Go back! Go back! He's gonna do it!" I pushed my way to see what was going on. As unpredictable as Herbert was, he literally climbed on to the window ledge and "leaped five stories to his DEATH!" I was stunned and shaken. At that moment, the police and ambulance arrived. I ran into the house to get the children and Mr. Singleton came out and said that he thought Mama was alive but was unconscious. There was blood everywhere. At first, I was too shocked to move.

"Daddy went out of the window..."

The police came in and I took them up to the apartment. Both doors back and front were locked, so they had to break in. I found the children right where the Lord had hidden them. Ethel Mae was crying, and in hysteria pointed at the window and said, "Daddy went out of the window (sobbing) Mama, Daddy went out of the window. My Daddy! My Daddy!" I just held her in my arms and we both cried. Herbie rolled from under the bed, trembling. We all just huddled together in silence crying and trembling, and trembling and crying.

## The Evening of January 30, 1923

People no doubt stood outside just talking about what had happened. There was blood on the snow where Herbert had died. It was there for many days frozen in ice as death's reminder. Mama was alive. She had been hit twice and had two flesh wounds. If it had not been for the steel boning in her corset, she would have been dead; and if it had not been for my hat, so would I. When Grace finally remembered that she bad her hat on, she took it off; and sure enough, the Lord's voice again rang out, "Put your hat on." There was a hole in her hat from the bullet the bullet that was intended for her head. Mother Hill again remarked, "A hat saved my life and steel boning saved my mama's life."

> "Now I praise you, brethren, that ye remember me in all things, and keep the ordinances, as I delivered them to you."

> "But I would have you know, that the head of everyman is Christ; and the head of the woman is the man; and the head of Christ is God."

> "But every woman that prayeth or prophesieth with her head uncovered dishonoreth her head: for that is even all one as if she were shaven."

> "For this cause ought the woman to have power onher head because of the angels."

> "Judge in yourselves: is it comely that a womanpray unto God uncovered?"

> I Corinthians 11

# From January 30, 1923 to February 1926

It seemed as though winter would never end. The house seemed dark and quiet. For many months, Ethel Mae was unable to sleep alone. She trembled all of the time. She was afraid to be alone, especially at night and especially in her room the room her father had decided to commit suicide in. "I took her for prayer and Bishop Lawson told me that the spirit of suicide and death was still in my house and had not finished its pernicious work." What more could happen? Grace must have wondered.

Here she was a young widow with two children. A full life ahead in one sense. She must have felt still bound, yet forever free. Grace was saved! SAVED! Set apart. Grace committed her life full time without interruption to God's plan for her life.

There was no doubt a period of mourning for the children and Grace as well. There was a period of readjustment and trauma. Along with Ethel Mae's being fearful there was young Herbert, who had his father's spirit, energy, and devilment. He always had the house in turmoil. He began to get harder to handle. In school he was acting out his frustrations and playing hooky. At home he was disobedient. He taunted Ethel Mae and nearly broke Grace's heart. Herbert was asunpredictable as his father. Then without a goodbye, without looking back, and without a warning, in February 1924, with a glint of mischievousness in his eyes the spirit of death caught him between two moving vehicles and rode with him to his death.

# PICTURE CODE

#1 – 6 THE CITADEL OF HOPE INFANT SCHOOL STAFF
Sisters Rosalie Thomas (deceased), Lottie Brown, Jacqualine Badger, Mother Grace Hill, Sister Cheryl Rivers and Sister Temple.

#7 - Mother Hill's Birthday Party. Shown with her are Mother Delphia Perry and other loved ones.

#8 - Sister Janie Richardson serves breakfast to Mother Hill.

#9 - Mother Pandora Williams, Mich. Presents roses to Mother Hill.

#10 - Mother Hill holding granddaughter, Bunny.

#11 - Mother Hill at Lady's B's Birthday Party.

#12 - Dear friend, Hilda Herring, with Mother Hill in Chicago, Illinois Convocation.

#13-15 Grandson Billy's three children.

#16 - Mother Hill's daughter, granddaughter, and great granddaughter.

#17 - Two of Mother Hill's brothers, George and Otho and their wives, Mattie and Ophelia

#18 - The home of the Willetts on Sanford Avenue, Flushing, Long Island, where Mother Hill used to work as an upstairs maid.

# Part Four

# The Morning Has Come

*March 1982*

# The Morning Has Come

"Weeping may endure for a night, but Joy cometh in the Morning"
Psalms 30:5

There is so much more about the life of Mother Grace Hill; but I will let those who know her best tell you in their own words what she still means to them in the following excerpts.

Mother Hill continues to live a triumphant life. Through many tragedies she has survived victoriously. Faithfully she withstood disappointments. Through adversity, she stood steadfast in the Apostle's Doctrine. Her life is an example STILL so that the destroyer of this age has been made a mockery of by her life. Mother Hill still endures through physical pain. Though stricken with Parkinson's disease, she still continues to be an encouragement to those who come to read, to sing, and to pray with her. She has yet to complain but gives God thanks and praise daily.

While visiting in her home I had the opportunity to share with her in her daily devotional period. Every day at noon, without fail, she began to pray aloud. There was no clock that let her know the hour, no nursemaid that said it is time to pray; but it was her habit, her way, her lifestyle to pray at noon; and her spirit made intercession for her. Her prayer summoned her nurse to cover her head for prayer.

Mother Grace Marie Hill lives the scripture in James 5 that reads: "Is there any sick among you? Let him call for the elders of the church; and let them pray over him, anointing him with oil in the name of the Lord: and the prayer of faith shall save the sick, and the Lord shall raise him up. The effectual, fervent prayer of a righteous man availeth much."

I am reminded of the story Mother Bonner related to me concerning a growth Mother Hill had which protruded almost 5 inches in width and almost 8 inches in length from the side of her neck. From 1943 to 1958, fifteen years, Mother Hill prayed that God would heal her. In June 1958 Mother Hill was staying with her daughter Ethel Mae in Detroit, she started down the stairs to the basement and accidentally slipped and fell over an ottoman and struck her face against the door loosening two of her teeth but causing no other injury. She was taken to the hospital for a check-up and it was discovered that the growth had become detached inside her neck. An incision was made and the growth, which was a calcium deposit was removed. Mother Hill waited on God for her healing 15 years! You might say a divinely inspired accident induced her healing.

So today with no medication for Parkinson's Disease due to the effects of such on the memory, Mother Hill refuses the very medication that would allow her physical activity; but which would deteriorate her memory simultaneously. So she continues to stand straight in a crooked society.

## March 6, 1982

Upon my departure, there is a feeling of sadness. For some reason I just don't want to go home not just yet.

It is as though some strong Godly spirit has me bound in 8-B. Tears begin to surface at my eyelid's edge. I look out of my bedroom study where I have spent the past week, gathering material, writing, praying and studying the life of Mother Grace Marie Hill, the mother of Ethel Mae Bonner.

There is a mist about the day, here in New York City. It is quiet still outside. I breathe and my breath stutters inside my chest. It is time. Time to go.

What have I come for? This is my thought upon arrival. Why me to do this task? And now, have I received what I had come for? Yes, I have received, and even more; I have done the most difficult thing, I have given. You ask, what could I have given to this Great Lady of God?

I gave my pride away to serve her, I gave my ears to hear her, I gave my mouth to keep silent as she prayed and spoke to God. I gave my mind to absorb the whole holy experience. I am trembling even now as I write, because truly I have seen God. As the mountains in Waterville Valley left me dumbfounded and in awe and fear so has this mountainous woman now hewn into a fragile frame.

I reached for her and said, Mother I must leave today. She said, "I thought you were leaving Saturday." I said, today is Saturday. I don't want to leave - for you have been a blessing to me. Mother,' may I kiss you goodbye?" She beams and her lips part to form a smile and she said so sweetly, "yes" and I put my lips against her brown face- the one God created in his own image, and I kissed her.

DEEP.
DEEP and Long.

She is warm still.

I said good-bye. Leaving, Mother, as she is affectionately called was like leaving home for the first time. I want to linger here with her for yet a little while; but God lifts me and carries me away in his spirit for now I must pass over into another mountain.

Slowly I walk to the elevator to go down and say goodbye to the dear one who sent for me, Mother Bonner. She had not been feeling well the entire week. We had celebrated her birthday with a dinner that I had so nervously prepared.

I sat with her each night, recording and writing. She had shared and entrusted me with her life's story. I had walked with her through the city, sat with her at the doctor's office, prepared small meals, did the dishes; and we drank tea together, something she rarely did. I do not take for granted those moments. I shall cherish the time with reverence.

I knocked on the door and went in. Bishop Bonner had just left. I was relieved. I didn't think I could bear being in the presence of the burning bush too! I said, "Well I've got to go." She had asked me to stay another week and to attend a birthday dinner in her honor. I was unable to stay. She reached for my hand, and held it firmly in hers, and thanked me. Little did she know, that my soul was panting. I said, "Thank you" and leaned over and stole a kiss. We both laughed, and I walked to the door. She, not being well, remained seated. I turned. She had on a long gown and her beautiful gray hair clung to her shoulders. She had a wide smile. I turned around one last time before closing the door and with my mind I took a picture of the moment.

My morning had come...

# Part Five

# A Living Legend

*Render therefore to all their dues, tribute to whom tribute is due; custom to whom custom1 fear to whom fear; honor to whom honor* (Romans 13:7).

Mother Hill resides in New York City with her daughter and son-in-law, Ethel Mae and William Lee Bonner. This small book is meant to be a Keepsake for all of those who know Mother Hill and those who will come to knowher from these pages.

This book is a gift from her daughter honoring her birthday, May 2, 1983. It will always serve as a memorabilia of Mother Hill's past and present. Her future belongs to God.

The following writings have been submitted by those who know her, love her and see her as a living legend.

**Mother Grace Hill**

Mother Grace Hill came to 13126 Orleans in the early 50's to stay with her daughter Ethel Mae Bonner and family. She fellowshipped with us here in Detroit. She was already saved and a member of Refuge COOLJC in N.Y., according to the word of God. She is a missionary and has done wonderful works for the Lord. She had made many visits here before she had decided to come and live. Mother Hill is a beautiful person in the Lord. She always had something to say about the Lord. She was very stern, but sweet and had no respect of persons. I love her. Mother Hill and I had traveled together, roomed together at convocations. We also lived together under the same roof. She was a great help to you, if you would accept it. She helped me many times. Mother Hill believes in prayer and is a praying woman who would expound the words of the Lord beautifully and with the anointing.

She returned to New York in the middle 70's. Detroit was her home while she was here. She would teach the missionaries every noonday. I was president of the missionaries at the time and I asked Bishop Lawson to let her be my instructor. Mother Hill was a person who was direct from the fountain right where everything was, and we were taught more about the body of Christ. She didn't belong to any choirs but she loved to sing congregational songs. I think one of her favorite songs was "I come to the garden alone." She believed in correcting you if you needed correcting. Mother Hill wouldn't have it on her mind knowing she could have told you differently and didn't.

If you came to her for comfort about a problem, she used the Word as a source of comfort for you. She mostly used the Word rather than relying on her own knowledge. There should be more Grace Hills around today. The most important thing I learned from her as a missionary was to be more spiritual.

I can remember, as a young missionary for the Lord, I found myself copying her movements. I quickly had to ask the Lord to give me my own individuality. She was a wonderful person to sit and listen to. She had much to say.

As I understand it, even though her companion didn't agree with her being saved, Mother Hill went on anyway and went through pure torment. Yet, she didn't slacken with the Lord. She told the Lord that if it cost her, her life and her family, she wasn't gonna give him (the Lord) up. And it almost cost her that; but yet and still she kept holding on to the Lord.

One of her favorite sayings was: "Salvation is free - everything else will cost you."

Others have told me she was a very spiritual minded woman. A woman of the word and she lived just that way - by the word.

Romans the 6th Chapter was one of her favorite chapters to teach - explaining how we had become new creatures in Christ. She was an exceptionally good teacher. Mother Hill also loved to cook and sell food. She was a very faithful woman. If there was a job to do, Mother Hill stayed until it was finished. When she had something to do, she didn't like any foolishness - no monkeying around to be exact.

**Combined work of Mother Hudson, Mother Hall, (and others)**
**Compiled by Sister Joyce Ursery**

*Who can find a virtuous woman? For her price is far above rubies.* (Proverbs 31:10)

Mother Hill worked faithfully in the church as a Sunday School teacher. She was a member of the Senior Choir, a member of the 'Go Forth Auxiliary' and served in many other capacities Her pastor, the late Bishop R.C. Lawson, saw in her the making of a great leader. He licensed Mother Hill as a missionary. He saw in her, the making of a great leader. Her license designated her a 'praying missionary'; and for fifteen years, she was in charge of the noonday prayer service.

Mother Hill served as the New York State Secretary and as the New York State Mother. In 1951, Mother Hill moved to Detroit, Michigan. Before leaving she saw the need for expansion of the work and development of leadership. So, she organized the first State Mothers' Assistants to carry on in her absence. They were, Sister Margaret Leader, Sister Lillian McCarty, Sister Bessie Jones and Sister Beulah Turner. Under Mother Hill's administration, the New York State 'Sick Aide' was established, the New York State Missionary Choir organized and also the Memorial Stamp was created with the words of our late Bishop and his picture:

"Remember the words I have spoken unto you while I was present with you."

Mother Hill was also a writer and her article on "The Value of a Dime" was published in the Contender for the Faith. She is a Mother in deed, example, patience, dedication, faithfulness, endurance and in prayer. She taught the missionaries. She reproved when it became necessary to do so; yet in her gentle manner, you accepted it, determined to overcome and go forward. It is a blessing to all whose lives have touched by this noble woman· of God. To know Mother Hill is to love her. Theseare the highlights of a beautiful life.

**Sister Dorothy Richardson Bronx, New York**

I, Wilhemina W. Wheatley met Mother Jones in the early part of my saved life. We were very fond of each other. She was indeed a Mother in Israel.

We often spent lots of time together. I found her to be a loving mother that gave good instruction and godly counsel which I enjoyed very much.

Mother Jones' sister, Sister Taylor and I used to meet together at our all-night prayer service. Sister Taylor lived in Corona, Long Island and would come over every Saturday night to the prayer service.

We looked forward to the Saturday night service. The Lord blessed us in these meetings- also at our noonday prayer service before Grace was saved.

Mother Jones and I would meet together and very often we would talk -sometimes a long time with each other.

After one noonday prayer service, Mother Jones invited me to her home to have lunch with her and Ethel. Ethel was a small child at that time. At the time appointed, Mother Jones, Ethel and I went to the house after prayer service. After entering Mother Jones' home, she and I sat talking, Mother Jones said to Ethel, "Ethel darling, go in the front and play with your dolly, I want to talk to Sister Wheatley. "In her talking, she expressed a feeling to me about her daughter Grace, and how she wished so much that she'd be saved. So often in our meetings she would request that the saints pray that her daughter Grace would be saved.

In our talking she expressed her feeling that someday something would happen to Grace. She expressed to me how she felt about her son-in-law. I tried to persuade her that it didn't have to be like that. She said, "Ob Sister Wheatley, I can't get away from this feeling that something will surely happen. You don't know my son-in-law." said, "Mother Jones we will join you in prayer." At our next missionary monthly meeting, I told the other mothers about the conversation Mother Jones and I had. I felt deeply impressed by the words Mother Jones had spoken. I said, "Let us pray with Mother Jones."

One day after prayer service Mother Jones called me outside the church. When I got outside, Mother Jones said, "Sister Wheatley, this is my daughter Grace." We were happy to meet each other. Grace said to me, "My mother often speaks of you to me." And I said, "Your mother would be so happy if you would get saved." She said, "Maybe soon." I replied, "I hope so."

Not long after that she got saved while her husband was away. Mother Jones came to the noon- day service and asked the saints to pray. She had a dread that something would happen.

After the husband returned, he didn't permit them to leave the apartment which upset Mother Jones very much. We continued in prayer and one Sunday evening, after a missionary meeting, Mother Bell, Mother Campbell, Mother Williams and other missionaries were talking about Mother Jones, Grace and Ethel. The missionaries appointed me at this time to go see Sister Grace - just to make a visit and come back; and they would be waiting and praying for my return.

While going toward Fifth Avenue, I heard the voice of God telling me not to go. I turned around and looked and looked. I said within my-self no one knew where I was going except the missionaries at the church who were waiting for me to return. I turned back and went to the church. They were surprised to see me return so soon. Mother Bell asked, "What happened, Wilhemina, that you got back so soon?" I said, "The Lord told me not to go."

Mother Campbell said to Mother Bell, "I believe her, let us go." They went to see about Sister Grace while the rest of us stayed and prayed for their safe return. When they returned they were weeping and were greatly surprised to find things as they were.

Mr. Smith was raging and said to them that he didn't respect a word that they were saying but he did recognize the gray in their hair. If it wasn't for the gray on their head he would have kicked them down the stairs! They were so happy that I obeyed the voice of God and returned back safe.

After their return, we bonded ourselves together in prayer around the clock ·for God's deliverance.

Mother Jones fasted until her complexion changed. We always encouraged her that some way the Lord would deliver.

She knew he had a gun and worst of all.

**Humbly submitted,**
**Mother Wilhemina W. Wheatley**

*All the days of my appointed time will I wait, till my change come.* (Job 14:14)

May 10, 1981, the Greater Refuge Temple, Senior Missionary Department, under the direction of the president, Sister Dorothy Anderson - presented a program, "This Is My Story", in honor of Mother Grace Hill.

Those that served on the editorial of her life were Sister F. Jenkins, Sister I. Harris, Sister E. Pauldin, Sister E. Pickett, Sister M. Skirritt, Sister F. Brown, Sister M. Durant, Sister D. J. Hughley and Sister L. Reid.

This is a capsule of the information that was gathered:

As it was mentioned Mother Hill had had a growth on the side of her neck for fifteen years. It was her way to wait. She waited for God to save her in 1923. She waited for God to deliver her from the hands of an angry husband, whom she loved. She waited for God to free little Ethel Mae from the spirit of fear and suicide that remained in her home. Mother Hill waited for fifteen years for God to heal her body and she waits still, and patiently for the promise of deliverance from Parkinson's' disease.

It was accounted that during the 1948 National Convention, that Mother Hill wrote three promises in a notebook. She had prayed for healing and in her petition one of her promises to the Lord was that, she would render any money she had towards the educational programs in the foreign field. Perhaps this is why Ethel Mae's heart belongs to Africa and why she believes so strongly and works so diligently within the Women's Council - teaching educators to educate.

## Conjecture

It was in Detroit. A day in June, 1958. No doubt it was a beautiful day. The sun was dancing on the plants on the windowsill. Mother Hill had come to Detroit to stay with young William Lee and Ethel Mae in their home. She was always busy doing something. Whether it was at noonday prayer, talking with the missionaries, encouraging the young ministers, reprimanding the little ones in love; or dusting around the house. She believed, no doubt, the scripture in paraphrase ' "If you don't work, you certainly don't intend to eat!"

Even though Mother Hill had gained weight and the extremely large growth on the side of her neck had slowed her down a bit; she had not stopped. On this particular day (let's call it the day of deliverance}, Mother Hill had started down the stairs to the basement. She had turned the light on; but her eyes bad not yet adjusted from going to the bright light of the sun upstairs, to the darkness that emerged from the basement. Satan must have thought it to be a perfect time to trip Mother· Hill.But "who is as great a God as our God?" The Lord has Hisown way of deliverance; and what the devil put in her waywas an ottoman. Now an ottoman is an overstuffed foot- stool. As Mother Bill approached the door to the basementand began to descend the narrow passageway, first one step then...without warning, just as her eyes began to focus in the darkness, her foot bumped into the ottoman and for a split second she lost her balance. As she tripped over several stairs, bracing mightily, against the door and she tumbled a few steps down, crying out, I imagine, the name of Jesus.

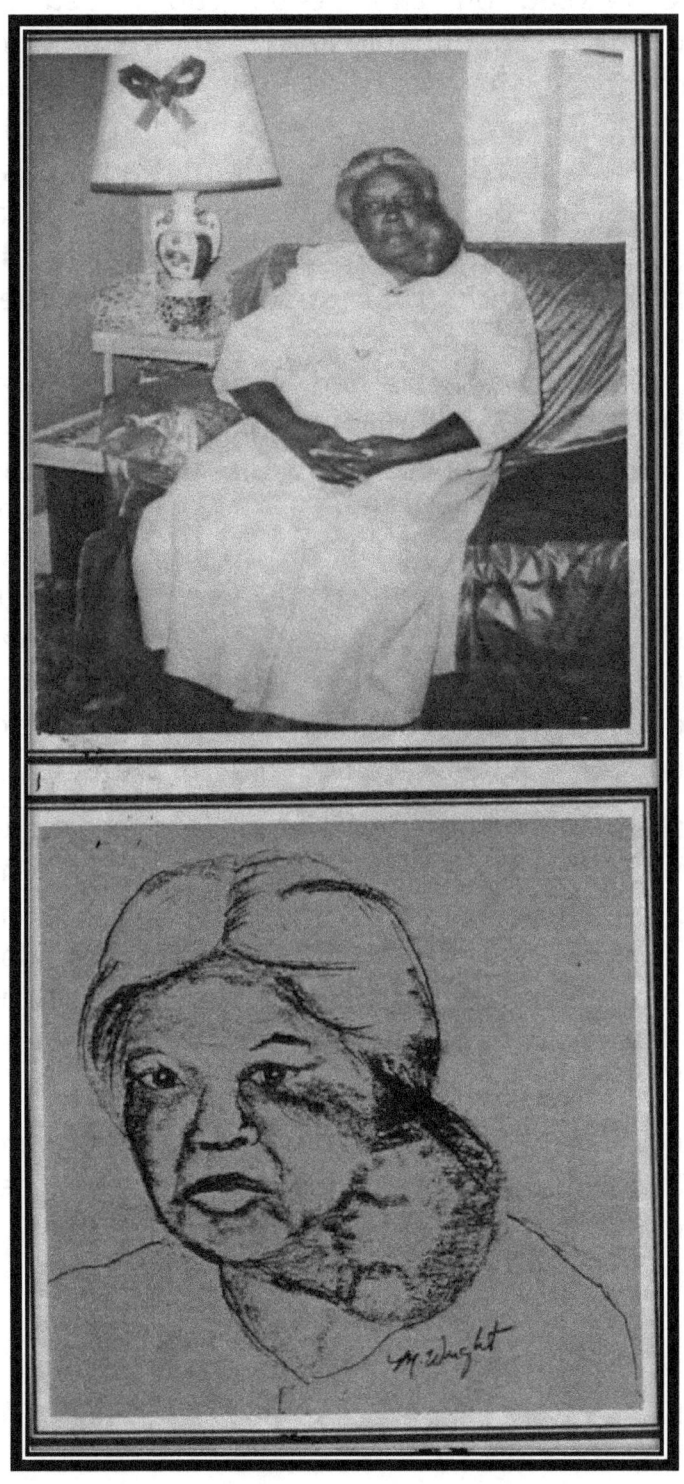

Artist: Mother Maudlin Wright
Mission Church Boston, MA

As she rested on the steps too dazed to move, her leg twisted, head throbbing and traces of blood surfacing from her mouth - she mumbled not one complaint against God. Mother Hill was immediately rushed to the hospital. The blow to her head from the door had loosened two of her teeth, but God had used this ensnarement as a time of miraculous deliverance. Due to the pain that had incurred from the fall, Mother Hill sought medical help, not for medication, nor for an operation - but more than likely for x-rays. It was determined that a very small incision in the side of her inflamed cheek would have to be made. For it was revealed, through the x-ray, that whatever the protrusion was, it had become detached and inflamed, probably from the fall and blow to her head. We know that God specializes in things that seem impossible. It was not the fall, nor was it the blow to her head from the door. It was the hand of God that reached down, blessed be the Name of God and touched His child, Grace Marie. He had heard her cry and answered her prayer of petition.

When the doctors opened the side of her face, a large, hard, fleshy substance was removed. It was not a tumor, nor was it malignant. It was an accumulation of calcium deposits that had settled there - so that God might get the glory. For He knew that Grace Marie would wait on him. She lived the scripture, "in your patience possess ye, your soul."

Someone said; that Mother Hill responded, "I'm so glad that I waited on the Lord." After fifteen years the Lord healed her of her affliction.

## This Mother Hill's Testimony:

"The hymn says, "If you hold out and wait on the Lord, you shall receive a just reward." I praise God today for all of his goodness and blessings. Truly God is great, and greatly to be praised. I thank him for being able to have noonday prayer service conducted in my home every day. Blessed be the name of God. They that trust in the Lord shall be as Mount Zion, which cannot be removed, but abideth forever; and they shall be like a tree planted by the rivers of water.

On this blessed Mother's Day, I would like to extend Holy Greetings to all of the Mothers that are present here today. Mother's Day in the United States is set aside to honor all motherhood and, by some gift or act of regard, to express love for one's Mother.

Anna Jarnia of Philadelphia is recognized as a founder of Mother's Day which, by an act of Congress in 1914, made the second Sunday in May, observable across the country. I am 89 years of age and I still have a desire to wait on the Lord, until my change comes. Blessed be the name of Jesus!

Mothers: give yourselves a lovely day. The kind that proves to be so filled with joy, that it turns into a precious memory. Remember, someone wishes you the best and thinks of you all year through. Happy Mother's Day.

**Mother Grace Hill**

**Mother Bonner holds the microphone for Mother Hill who is extending greetings to mothers on Mother's Day.**

In 1954 the following article entitled, The Value of a Dime, was written by Mother Hill and published in The Contender for the Faith.

A. According to metal value: 20 grams of copper equals 1 penny weight. 10 penny weight equals 1 dime.

B. According to buying value: In this day and time, its buying value is very small. It will not buy any substantial food such as a loaf of bread or a bottle of milk or any kind of meat. Years past it would buy these things and even a pair of stockings for a child and a yard of material or two or three yards of lace and many more useful articles. That's why Woolworth's 5 and 10 cents stores sprang up all over the country; but now these same articles cost five and six times as much.

C. When given to God for tithes; it has, now as in the past, and will in the future have, the same value. For in God there is no variableness, neither shadow of turning. His price and values always remain the same.

A tithe is one-tenth of what the Lord has prospered you; and it belongs to the Lord for the support of those who are ordained to labor in word and doctrine, that they may give their fulltime to the ministry. Many are hindered because we as saints fail to pay tithes in full as we should; and the pastors are bound on some job because of the need of sufficient funds to support their families. So the work of God is hindered and people of God are at fault. Malachi 3:10 says, "bring ye all the tithes and I will open the windows of heaven and pour you out a blessing that there shall not be room enough to receive it. I will rebuke the devourer for your sakes. So, God does not only give but he protects that which he has given; and his promise is to everyone that brings all the tithes, whether your tenth part is as much as someone else's or not. If He has prospered us with so much, He requires much of us, for the scripture says, "To whom much is given, much will be required." He rewards our giving according to our honesty in giving and not our abundance, as he rewards our service according to our faithfulness and not the amount of work that we do. Therefore, he said to the man that had the five and two talents and traded and gained another five and two talents more, "Well done thou good and faithful servant." Of the widow who cast in more than the others who gave of their abundance, He said she gave her living - all that she had. Consider these values and judge ye whether it is more profitable to you to keep and spend the dime or give it to God.

**MY TESTIMONY:**

While I was sitting in the auditorium of Refuge Temple during testimony service in the convention in New York, the song dropped into my heart, "When the Tithes are gathered in," I thought to myself, "The Lord wants me to testify about tithes." I failed to do so; and shortly the Bishop came in and sang the song, "When the Tithes Are Gathered In;" but said nothing about tithes. So to try to make right this mistake, I'm putting it in print. I believe it is right to pay tithes; and I pay them not only out of what I earn, but whatever way the Lord prospers me. I believe, too, that whatever the Church asks for in the way of an offering, it is right to give. Many times, it is not easy but that's what God wants, a sacrifice. Then when I'm sick or have a toothache I can look to the Lord and tell him I have no money for the doctor or the dentist. Many of us are to the contrary. We lay aside for the doctor and dentist and tell God we have no money for His work. It is wise to lay aside these emergencies; but let us not rob God to do so.

# Part Six

# Epilogue

# Acknowledgements by the author

I would like to take this opportunity to thank several people that have been instrumental during the construction of this task:

My Lord and Savior Jesus Christ for blessing us with the power of creative words.

Lady Grace Marie Hill, for possessing a life worth gold and worth writing about.

Mother Ethel Mae Bonner for selecting me to write the biography of this great woman.

## Special Appreciation To

Sister Elvina Dewberry for her excellent typing ability and patience with me during creative highs and lows.

Sister Maudlin Dewberry Wright for her beautiful calligraphy work.

Mother DyAnne Echols Moultrie (my beloved sister) for assisting in the editing.

Bishop H.A. Moultrie, my pastor who, when I wanted to give up, Said go ahead, go ahead, go ahead.

Thank you, Deacon Alexander Stewart, and especially Seymour Press for wanting to republish this book.

I wish Mother Bonner was here to see this dream come true!

# Acknowledgements

# by

# The First Lady's Daughter

Words cannot express the deep appreciation I feel for the labor of love performed by Sister CheVonceil Echols of Medford, Mass.

CheVonceil was in much the same position as Daniel was when he was requested by King Nebuchadnezzar to interpret a dream (Daniel 4:9) the details of which the king himself had forgotten. And just as God met Daniel's need in that unique situation, so God met Che's need in this situation which was equally as unique.

Over two years have passed since CheVonceil came to me in the Hyatt Regency in the National Convocation which met in North Carolina and asked for the "privilege" of writing the story of my life. I explained to her that the first chapter of the story of my life is really the life story of my mother.

I admire the courage with which CheVonceil took on thisHerculean task and the determination with which she heldon to it until the task was completed. For she did this in addition to all of her other numerous activities. If, after this ordeal, CheVonceil still deems it a "privilege," then you may expect a sequel to WILL THE REAL FIRST LADY, entitled THE FIRST LADY'S DAUGHTER.

I also appreciate all of the expert advice given me by Marty of Hamilton Copy Center and his typist, Louise, Mrs. Barbara Penn Atkins of Pica Systems Inc. and the assistance of Florence Lewis and Mary Durane of Refuge Temple.

I am well aware that this, by no means, is an exhaustive account of my mother's life; but it is the best that Sister Echols and I could do in so short a period of time. She and I both know that locked up in their hearts and minds of many are recollections, anecdotes, and memories about Mother Hill and the tremendous impact she had on the lives of those she touched. We hope that reading this book will motivate those people to make their identity known and to share with us what they know of this great woman of God, so that the second edition can be more comprehensive than the first.

GOD BLESS YOU - ONE AND ALL!

P.S. I must not close without thanking God for permitting Dr. Lois Anderson to come all the way to New York from Greensboro, North Carolina to board a Hudson River Dayline Boat on the same day that Refuge Temple did so, to recognize me from her girlhood memories of me as a child, to approach me as I walked on the middle deck, and to make her identity known to me after a half a century. The things that she and her friends shared with me in the Refuge Temple Pastor's Dining Room on the following day enabled me to write the final pages of this book.

I was blessed to have sharing this wonderful occasion with me, Mother Iona Johnson, the wife of the bishop who first called me "Lady Bonner," namely, Bishop Edwin Johnson of Trinidad and Sister Donetta Bryant, the secretary registrar of the R.C. LAWSON INSTITUTE OF LIBERIA LABORATORY SCHOOL to which I gave, by God's grace, three and one half years of my life and happy years they were!

Dr. Lois Anderson

Sister Bryant of Liberia, W. Africa

Friends of Dr. Anderson

Recapturing youth with Mother Grace Hill is Mother Bessie Jones, Mother Harriet Maloney, Sister Hattie Banks, and many other loved ones. Do you see yourself, your friends, your relatives?

Mother Hill with her three brothers Otho, George and Octave. Otho's son, "Little Octave and Mother Hill's daughter.

**Dear, dear Grandma: On her wedding day, Bunny pins an orchid on Dear Grandma before the ceremony in Detroit, Michigan.**

**Grandson, Billy sits with Dear Grandma at Bunny's New York wedding reception.**

**Mother Hill smiles as she holds the rough draft of her biography on September 9, 1983.**

# The Author

Dr. CheVonceil Echols is a charter member of the Mission Church of Our Lord Jesus Christ in Boston Massachusetts where she was a co-laborer with her sister Mother DyAnne and brother-in-law Apostle Henry A. Moultrie, II.

Dr. Echols has been a stalwart in her local church. She has served in various capacities. Missionary President, Women's Council president and was the tarry committee coordinator for over 25 years. She served as adult Sunday School Teacher, Youth for Christ Director, local and international counseling staff, praise team and lead singer, and has received numerous awards for her faithfulness.

She holds a B.S. degree in Education from North Carolina Agricultural and Technical State University in Greensboro, North Carolina. She received a M.Ed. in Counseling from Northeastern University, as well as a Ph.D. in Christian Counseling from Royal Priesthood Academy in San Antonio, Texas. She completed advance studies in education, social work and counseling at Boston University.

Dr. Echols is the published author of four books. This volume was commissioned by the late Dr. Ethel Mae Bonner through the Christ Publishing Company. The author is a retired licensed certified social worker andcertified teacher who lives in San Antonio Texas. She hasone son Lee, a daughter-in-law Angela and one grandson, Jaden.